SCORPIONS IN THE DARK

Doreen Gonzales

PowerKiDS
press

New York

Published in 2010 by The Rosen Publishing Group, Inc.
29 East 21st Street, New York, NY 10010

First Edition

Editor: Amelie von Zumbusch
Book Design: Julio Gil
Photo Researcher: Jessica Gerweck

Photo Credits: Cover Stephen Cooper/Getty Images; pp. 5, 9 Shutterstock.com; p. 6 © David A. Northcott/ Corbis; p. 10 © Theo Allofs/Corbis; p. 13 © ARCO/D. Usher/age fotostock; p. 14 © Michael & Patricia Fogden/Corbis; p. 17 © Joe McDonald/Corbis; p. 18 © Frans Lanting/Corbis; p. 21 J. Kim/Getty Images.

Library of Congress Cataloging-in-Publication Data

Gonzales, Doreen.
  Scorpions in the dark / Doreen Gonzales. — 1st ed.
    p. cm. — (Creatures of the night)
  Includes index.
  ISBN 978-1-4042-8100-4 (lib. bdg.) — ISBN 978-1-4358-3257-2 (pbk.) —
  IBSN 978-1-4358-3258-9 (6-pack)
  1. Scorpions—Juvenile literature. I. Title.
  QL458.7.G66 2010
  595.4'6—dc22

                                    2009002076

Manufactured in the United States of America

CONTENTS

Have you ever seen a scorpion? Scorpions are easy to recognize. They have long tails, which turn up at the ends. Scorpions also have two body parts, called pedipalps, which end in clawlike pincers.

However, people do not often see scorpions. Most scorpions are **nocturnal**. They hide during the day and hunt for food at night.

All scorpions are arachnids. Arachnids are small animals with two basic body parts and eight legs. Spiders and ticks are also members of the arachnid family. As many arachnids do, scorpions eat other animals.

Scorpions have stingers at the ends of their tails. These arachnids often curl their tails above their bodies to scare off animals that want to eat them.

There are more than 1,000 kinds of scorpions. The smallest scorpions are only 1.6 inches (4 cm) long, but the long-tailed African scorpion grows to be 8 inches (20 cm) long! Scorpions live in many places around the world. Most scorpions live in deserts, but some live in rain forests, in caves, or on mountains.

No matter where scorpions live, they almost always find somewhere to hide during the day, while other animals are out looking for food. Many scorpions spend their days under stones, leaves, or tree bark. Other scorpions stay in underground dens, called burrows.

This scorpion is a desert hairy scorpion. These large scorpions live in the deserts of Mexico and the southwestern United States.

Pedipalps and Pincers

Most scorpions are black, brown, or dark yellow. Their colors **camouflage** these arachnids, making them hard to see both during the day and at night.

Scorpions have eyes, mouths, and pedipalps on the front of their bodies. Scorpions use the clawlike ends of their pedipalps to catch and hold things. Scorpions have four pairs of legs. There are very **sensitive** feelers beneath the last pair of a scorpion's legs. All scorpions have sharp stingers on the tips of their tails. Some scorpions hold their tails over their heads, while other scorpions hold theirs to the side.

You can see the pedipalps and pincers on this flat rock scorpion. Flat rock scorpions live in southern Africa. Their flat bodies let them hide in small spaces between rocks during the day.

A Scorpion's Sting

Scorpions often sting their **prey**. Sometimes, scorpions add **venom** to their sting. The venom comes from a special place near their stingers. The venom can kill an animal or make it stop moving long enough for a scorpion to eat it. About 20 kinds of scorpions have venom strong enough to be a danger to the people they sting.

Scorpions also sting animals that **attack** them. Several nocturnal animals, such as owls, bats, and lizards, eat scorpions. Some scorpion eaters will break off a scorpion's tail to keep from getting stung. There are also a few animals that are not hurt by scorpion venom.

Meerkats often eat scorpions. These African animals even teach their pups to hunt scorpions by letting them catch and eat scorpions that have already had their stingers bitten off.

WHAT'S THAT I FEEL?

Most scorpions hunt at night, when it is too dark for them to see. Therefore, they find their food with touch. Scorpions have special hairs all over their bodies. These hairs sense small movements in the air and on the ground. Scorpions can feel movements made more than 1 foot (30 cm) away.

Scorpions are quiet hunters. Many scorpions sit still in the dark and wait for prey to come near. In fact, some scorpions just stick their heads out of their burrows and wait for prey to pass by! A few scorpions search for prey. When scorpions feel prey nearby, they catch it with their pedipalps.

This scorpion has caught a spider. Along with special hairs, scorpions also use sensors called pectines and slits, or thin openings, to sense when their prey is nearby.

DRINKING TO EAT

Scorpions spend their days resting. When they come out at night to hunt, scorpions generally catch other nocturnal animals. They like to eat **insects**, spiders, and other scorpions. Large scorpions sometimes also eat bigger animals, such as lizards and mice.

Scorpions are excellent hunters. However, they have a strange method of eating their food. Once they have caught their prey, scorpions tear it into little pieces. Scorpions make special **enzymes** that they spread on their prey. This makes the prey break down into a **liquid**. Then, scorpions use their tiny mouths to drink up their now liquid prey. Scorpions spit out any fur or dry body parts they cannot drink.

This scorpion from the African country of Namibia is eating a dune cricket. Crickets are an important food for many kinds of scorpions.

Mother scorpions have live babies, called scorplings. Some kinds of scorpions have only 6 scorplings, while others can have more than 100.

Newborn scorplings climb onto their mothers' backs. The scorplings stay there for several weeks, eating food that their mothers catch. The babies soon grow out of their first **exoskeletons**. When a scorpling's exoskeleton becomes too small, it breaks open and the baby crawls out. Then, a new exoskeleton grows around the scorpion. This is called molting. After their first molt, most scorplings leave their mothers to begin life on their own. Scorpions molt five or six more times before they are fully grown.

Baby scorpions, such as these ones resting on their mother's back, tend to be much lighter in color than adult scorpions are.

STAYING COOL

Many scorpions live in hot places. These scorpions stay cool by hiding in burrows during the heat of the day. The scorpions come out only after the Sun sets and the air cools. Hiding from the Sun also helps scorpions keep water in their bodies. All animals need water. However, most scorpions do not drink much water. Instead, they get water from the liquids in their prey.

Scorpions do not eat often, though. Since they do not move around much, scorpions generally use little **energy**. This means they do not need to catch prey often. In fact, scorpions can live for a year without eating!

This scorpion comes from the hot, dry Kalahari Desert, in southern Africa. The Kalahari is home to several kinds of scorpions.

WATCH OUT!

Even though some scorpions have venom that is strong enough to kill, few people die from scorpion stings. Scorpion stings do hurt, though, and they can make a person very sick. Anyone who is stung by a scorpion should stay calm and call a doctor. Doctors have **medicines** that can keep even the strongest venom from hurting someone.

Still, people who live around scorpions should watch out for them. People need to be careful around rocks or wood piles where scorpions might hide. They should shake out their clothes before putting them on and check their beds before climbing into them.

Scorpions that live near people often hide in shoes. If you visit or live in a place where scorpions can be found, check your shoes for scorpions before putting them on.

Scorpions After Dark

Are there any scorpions living around you? You can find out by using a special light called a black light. This kind of light makes scorpions glow in the dark! **Scientists** who study scorpions often use black lights to watch scorpions catching prey and digging burrows.

Many people keep scorpions as pets. Though scorpions make cool pets, it is also important for there to be plenty of scorpions living in the wild. In some places, there would be too many insects if there were no scorpions around to eat them. Animals that eat scorpions, such as owls, meerkats, and coyotes, need these arachnids in order to live. Scorpions are an important part of our world!

GLOSSARY

ATTACK (uh-TAK) To start a fight with.

CAMOUFLAGE (KA-muh-flahj) To hide by looking like the things around something.

ENERGY (EH-nur-jee) The power to work or to act.

ENZYMES (EN-zymz) Matter made by cells that causes changes to other matter.

EXOSKELETONS (ek-soh-SKEH-leh-tunz) The hard coverings on the outside of animal bodies that hold and guard the soft insides.

INSECTS (IN-sekts) Small animals that often have six legs and wings.

LIQUID (LIH-kwed) Matter that flows.

MEDICINES (MEH-duh-sinz) Drugs that doctors give you to help fight illness or when you are hurt.

NOCTURNAL (nok-TUR-nul) Active during the night.

PREY (PRAY) Animals that are hunted by another animal for food.

SCIENTISTS (SY-un-tists) People who study the world.

SENSITIVE (SEN-sih-tiv) Able to see or feel small differences.

VENOM (VEH-num) A poison passed by one animal into another through a bite or a sting.

INDEX

A
animal(s), 4, 7, 11, 15, 19, 22
arachnids, 4, 8, 22

B
bodies, 4, 8, 12, 19

E
ends, 4, 8
enzymes, 15
exoskeleton(s), 16

F
feelers, 8
food, 4, 7, 12, 15–16

front, 4, 8

I
insects, 15, 22

L
legs, 4, 8
liquid(s), 15, 19

M
medicines, 20

P
part(s), 4, 15, 22
pedipalps, 4, 8, 12
people, 4, 11, 20, 22

pincers, 4, 8
prey, 11–12, 15, 19, 22

S
scientists, 22
spiders, 4, 15

T
tail(s), 4, 8, 11
ticks, 4

V
venom, 11, 20

WEB SITES

Due to the changing nature of Internet links, PowerKids Press has developed an online list of Web sites related to the subject of this book. This site is updated regularly. Please use this link to access the list: www.powerkidslinks.com/cnight/scorpion/